Kenza Lakouiri

LOVE THE WORLD

Kenza Lakouiri

LOVE THE WORLD

Behave simply

JustFiction Edition

Imprint

Cover image: www.ingimage.com

Publisher:
JustFiction! Edition
is a trademark of
Dodo Books Indian Ocean Ltd., member of the OmniScriptum S.R.L Publishing group
str. A.Russo 15, of. 61, Chisinau-2068, Republic of Moldova Europe
Printed at: see last page
ISBN: 978-620-3-57861-4

PRESENTATION

- KENZA L.
- PAGES: xx PAGES
- LANGUAGE : ENGLISH
- TITLE : LOVE THE WORLD !
- AREA : POETRY
- STYLE : POEMS
- SUMMARY: Poetry texts, turning the world to a love world and giving hope to those that has none. There is always something positive in life, try to find it!

WAVING TIMES

FOR A THOUSAND YEAR!

I love you,

Crossing borders to meet you,

I've never been helpless,

Time got to kill me full,

Love was never hard for me,

Nothing could be like this whisper,

A smile crossing my feelings,

Loving you so easily,

I just get it.

I was blind,

Nothing was planned,

Crossing borders for nothing,

Now, I have a reason

Even everything is a dream.

This is my dream!

The only one,

A thousand year,

To get one love!

UNDERGROUND

Possessive to Negative,

I've been through the light,

I keep living the dark,

None has its rights,

You're a label,

You have the power,

You keep saying,

You're protecting me,

I've found you,

At the corner of my eyes,

I am so famous to be no one,

I am so proud to be you,

Fame made me selfish,

Cauz' you sang like nobody,

Are you even real?

BROKEN FACES

You were hidden,

At the years to see me,

My son, my daughter, mu everything,

For one simple reason, a life

All the lack of strength,

My Up & Down,

I've seen the light so many times,

To see you shine,

I didn't know, you're here!
would you give me a chance?

Would it be possible, to see again?

I try and I will,

You're my voice,

So, I am gonna find you

I wanna see you to smile,

Smile open heart again,

w/o doubts, failure & block

I wanna be here,

Leave my voice print.

Look at me, I am not yours

I feel OK, to see you cry

Maybe I am right, maybe I am wrong,

None could know,

This is your choices to see the light,

Underneath your beautiful,

There is always a hidden side,

I've told you to stay away from me,

My life is settled up,

I am a stranger,

Figuring out what life is,

Change is yours, make it or leave it,

I am not your Motherhood,

I am a simple human being,

I ahev to travel again,

My safety is out there!

LIGHTS & NIGHTS

Lights and Nights,

All day long,

I saw you brother,

I thought you were blind,

I found the family all diamonds,

With no luck to be here,

So, I crafted my image in your mind,

To give me your luck,

Your change and your face joy.

Your sister appreciated it,

Because she saw her family,

One day like that,

I was here to bounce.

To collapse your brother & sister hood,

To give you more,

But your father is a shit.

Oh! I'll take to myself,

I am gone to be a king.

Shut DOWN!

Sshut down,

One, two, three times,

My watch was working,

My life was running,

All is going forward,

Killed by people,

You'll feel free,

I saw you suffering,

You're my close to heart,

So, I begged to see you in Peace!

REBORN

I was Moroccan,

I died for this country,

So, I reborn American

Now, time to believe again

Another love to try,

New people to see,

Now, it's a new time

A clock is turning again,

To be Human, to be a phoenix,

All is here to make it,

I am surrounded to be me,

I am gone stand for life.

She's the truth,

Of human destroy,

It destroys climate,

Hearts & Lives,
Stop the war,

To be in Peace.

BEFORE YOU!

I was lost, empty

Alone in my bed,

I was a pic in this world,

Because of you, I am moving

Moving to see you,

I felt complete,

I saw here different,

I loved you so much,

No more memories,

You betrayed me to the bone,

I did a lot, to make you happy

You're on your track now,

w/o me, we're apart forever.

To not see you again,

I say Goodbye,

No more mercy, No more Hello!

No war, No Salam,

It's over, we're done.

TRY

All is moving,

Everything is gone,

Never enough, any try

Flowers in the bone,

Acapella Story,

I've never been there,

I leave to live a life,

I found myself Home,

There & here, you're so precious

Take care of yourself,

We're made to match,

We're gonna be together,

I feel so secure,

I don't wanna be here,

So deep to see you.

N.Y. & L.A. are coming,

They will be soon in my life,

To see you happy,

To love you again,

To be together,

To be TRUE,
Going back Home,

One Goodbye!

We're Free.

HERO

I am Hero to be alone,

Love is all around,

US is calling Night & Day,

My sorrow is already there,

My life is done,

I am gonna be there,

For a while, for a moment,

We're a family,

When I see you,

I feel happy,

I love to give you a hug,

None has your courage,

Your strength to smoke the carpet.

Nght & Day, me & you,

F...king ourselves in Miror-sky,

Hugs & loves,

No more cry,

Only shinning lights,

Aston Martin iis one lifetime,

No more mercy, no more sorry.

ONE BROKEN STRING!

One broken string,

It's enough to be born,

Maybe you're simple,

I feel complicated,

All was done,

You're still not satisfied,

I am a disease,

To see you cry,

I did my best,

Our live is broken,

All efforts are gone,

To survive, to reborn,

Now, it's time to say Goodbye!

Our love,

No more possible,

Even a hug, not considered

I decided to leave,

Keeping that ring for another life,

I would like to feel happy,

So, Time to leave.

Damned, she's good

Steps, I feel Happy

None has my skills,

None could see the truth,

Life has another meaning,

Just listening, no more!

Sorry, I've been here before,

Time wasted, to be TRUE.

THE VOICE

Blocked within my legs,

I feel secure and Happy,

I do my Homework,

I love to believe in,

You're no chance to see,

You're not done to survive,

I feel you inside me,

I love, I feel, I see

I can't give you more,

You're done,

My time is waisted,

To see, to cry, to drive,

I wanna go back home,

I look at my breast,

My feelings are empty.

I took my ticket,

The angel-sky,

To give faith or happiness,

Someone saw it & they want it,

So bad, to hope not see me crying

They're waiting for me,

Because they love me,

w/o any conditions.

This is it,

I gave you all,

My last is for the one,

The most beauty in life,

To see the light in my heart,

I love to see me,

I would like to see that,

Now, time to say Goodbye!

I knock my US door,

So easy, so opened,

My home country, my heart

Where has secret for me,

They want me to see their smile,

They look after me every single day.

L.A. is dangerous,

So, it's me!

I am ready to leave,

A new life to come,

A new world is ready,

To be with me, to be 1

In everything, protected

From open doors,

I do, I like you,

We're gonna make it yours.

THE LIGHT

If I turn on the light,

I would be very simple,

I will be quiet & strong,

I feel freedom & love,

All what I need to be me,

So easy to be tough,

A little ears in big ones,

It hurts to take you down,

You're right to be wrong,

You're complicated to get different,

We're changing you to be me,

Loosing control of my car,

In my front-door, to be weak

I don't lnow what happened.

I saw you crazy,

To loose you forever,

My voice is so loud now,

Noone has to hear it,

This is what you're looking for.

SPECIAL MOMENTS

SOMETIMES

Sometimes,

Little things are most beautiful,

All is going forward by itself,

To get this high top of friendly,

I feel secure, despite of circumstances

Life has a meaning,

The source is identified,

Time to get your arms down,

The look from outside,

To destroy the Hidden Side!

CROSS OVER & OVER

I feel me & you,

Crossing streets like a Monday,

Every single moment is a laugh,

You're all my upcoming sunny days,

I don't need money or work,

I wanna just be happy, my home

For Tomorrow, for now on,

A crossing bridge to breathing,

A new Salam, like none before

I love to see you smile,

I swear to keep you alive,

Heart & Soul, are a match

We're here again,

Are u ok?

Or I got turn around for a while?

Take a decision, let me know!

SALAM!

A shallow,

Glancing to the top line,

I was here to keep safe,

Every moment of ife,

Nothing's defined in your Name,

But none is hidden from all,

The boat is moving on,

Going forward,

The other river side.

A HEALER

A thousand year,

I am healing you,

I feel concerned,

Even it's a dream,

This is my dream,

My ring,

My love,

I am not sharing,

I am alone in this.

I feel to be free,

I love to see me,

I care to understand,

My ring is so tough,

My education is simple.

My brain is a heartbreak,

I meant to be closer,

To the sky, to the sea,

Being desperate,

At the last point.

You came from nowhere,

Expectations to be heard,

I was so clear,

Clear-up my memory,

Dust so heavy,

To see the love …

MAWAZINE, Please!

Music is turning,

Public shaving,

Undercover names,

All is here!

Being someone or none,

Calls are made for me,

Are you available to share?

HASSAN II is here to clap,

No more lies, I sware.

So precious,

Smiles all around,

Taking part of the quation,

Being part of this world,

No more marriage,

Sharing beds is enough for me.

Doing sport,

Smiling Fake,

Doing business,

No more family.

I'd love to see you,

I would like to be here,

No more, No more, Only 'YES'

NO BACK-UP!

I've been here before,

All was undertaken by me,

It was obvious that easy,

They were blind to see it,

I've said it, No more

You're taken so many steps back,

One forward is enough,

To destroy all strings.

I love you all, to hate you

Tears are cooling,

To give you one reason,

Four prints to take you down,

I am the DOG,

You're the queen.

I love to see you cry,

I win all the time,

You're losing Now!

TRAVELLING

SOBER DIFFERENT

I was normal,

One night stand out,

Change was here,

I didn't know,

Someone chase me,

My legs opened up,

Al feelings did come out,

I felt insecure,

Lost & complicated,

Our home was no more home,

Promises were made,

To revenge differently,

Don't stop him,

Just keep watching after me.

The break is my story,

To never forget,

I am who I am,

You can't destroy me, I'll shut you down.

BEFORE YOU

I was here to relax,

I feel happy to ignore,

My silence was killing you,

My faith was out there,

Love never left me,

Hidden to keep true & beautiful,

I love yourself,

Guiding was the only way,

Nobody can touch it,

I don't have to fear,

All is written simply,

Face to face,

I am another one.

Almost there to see,

All was simple,

They took me down,

So I have to be an angel sky,

I finished my work.

NO TIME FOR ANYONE

Talking is no more possible,

I am locked away,

To give you faith in yourself,

They're all working together,

For the same purpose,

I love to see their failure

Pushing is down,

Now, it's no more possible

We're done sa far,

To see you cry & weak,

Time to step on your feet.

CRASH

I was here,

Different world,

Single thought,

I loved the deepest,

I've shared everything,

I did it for real,

No backup plans,

All was defined for me,

Reality was mine.

HUMAN

I slept with a man,

Different categories,

No love in the picture,

To be here indeed, to leave

They're all going crazy,

To keep you alive,

I need to chest,

I look up to you down.

I hide all the best things,

Kept myself hidden,

To give you Hope,

You're looking for,

Trying is not possible,

You did it,

Need to rest and bring it out.

THE LAST CALL

Travelling all the way long,

I felt daisy, unhappy, confused,

Considering time, it was heavy

Bones tired, nerves creepy,

Never seen me tired,

So all questions went up,

I wasn't here anymore,

Lost myself for a cigarette,

Drunk a bottle of wine,

I've seen all dirty places,

Discovered the other Morocco,

Never new it was even existing.

By now, all is clear

Time flies by to forgive HOPE,

Keeping me safe & smile,

I am about to see you,

Again in my bed laughing,

Live my hand bag.

Talking to everyone,

Phone calls were so heavy,

Zagoura was here for the best,

Models, photographs, Game-boy,

No more chocolate, only wine

No see you, only Goodbyes.

It took me years to see purpose,

Nothing is in it, a lost piercing

In your mouth, trumped me

Down to UP, we're over!

I love you all,

W/O any close friendship,

Time stopped,

Life was no more possible,

Taxi is your Home,

Travelling again to L.A.

SINGING

Sing, Sing,

Find your way to speak,

I am singing the whole day,

Signature is vocalist,

I love to cry inside,

Laugh outside,

Crazy about happiness,

All is captured in one Note,

To give you purpose,

Slip out of my face,

I am alone in this world,

Unique in my style,

Trembling about levels,

Stable when decided,

Giving you the sound requested.

SUMMARY

POETRY

WAVING TIMES

1. For A thousand year
2. Underground
3. Broken Faces
4. Look at me, I am not yours
5. Lights & Nights
6. Shut Down!
7. Reborn
8. Before You
9. Try
10. Hero
11. ONE BROKEN STRING
12. THE VOICE
13. CROSS OVER
14. A HEALER

SPECIAL MOMENTS

15. THE ORIGIN
16. MAWAZINE, Please!
17. No BACK-UP!
18. Kenza FOSSIL
19. DIVERGENT
20. GOODBYE MY LOVERS
21. OH! MY GOD
22. TAKE BACK YOUR LOVE
23. SWIP ACTIVITY
24. MY GREEN EYES
25. SHUT DOWN!
26. LOOK AT ME, I AM NOT YOURS
27. THE WORLD, I APOLOGIZE
28. CROSSING FEAR
29. RESURRECTION
30. SECOND CHANCE

TRAVELLING

BIBLIO

- I AM A SURVIVAL poems
- BAROQUE WORLD
- POESIE BAROQUE
- CAMELEONINE

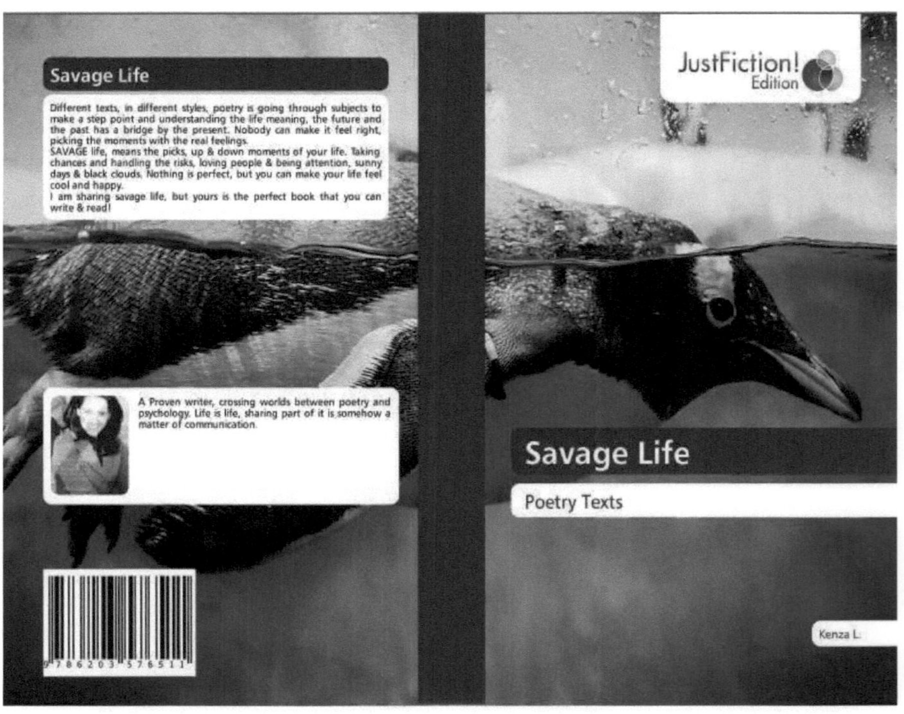

CONTACTS

Twitter : @laestycia

Instagram : @kencool26

Linkedin : #laplumekenzaouite

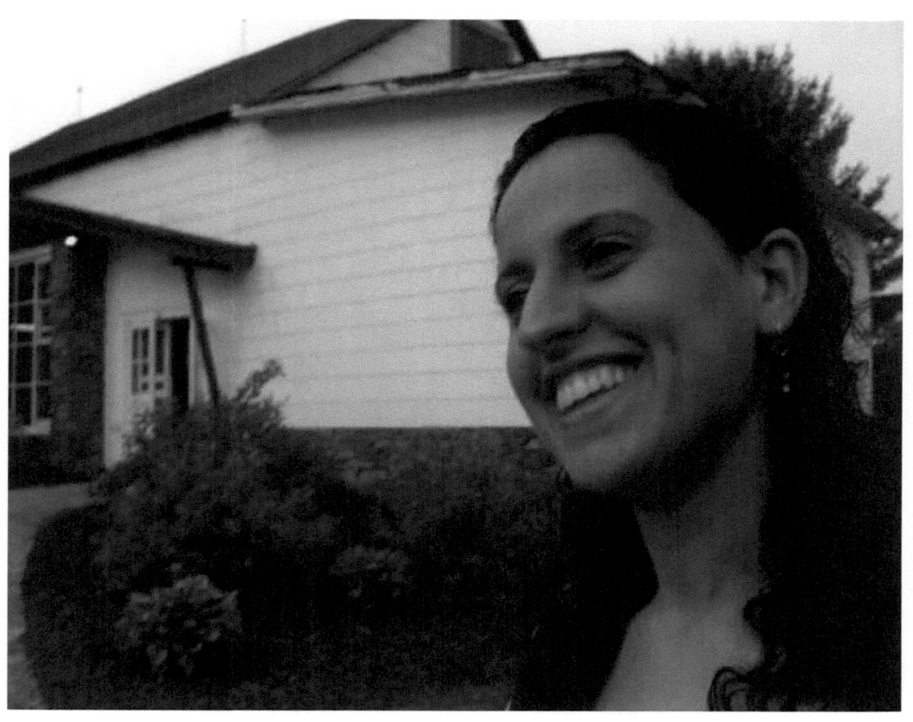

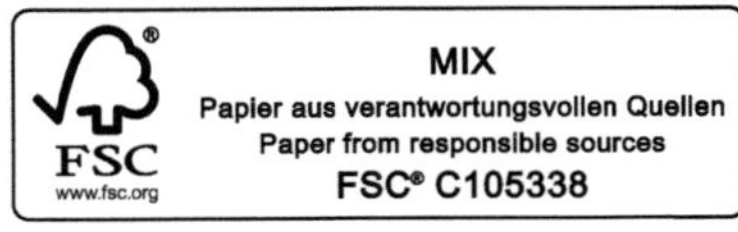

Printed by Books on Demand GmbH, Norderstedt / Germany